MYSTERIES OF HISTORY

THE MYSTERY OF
AREA 51

by Barbara Krasner

WARNING

U.S. Air Force Installation

It is unlawful to enter this area without permission of the Installation Commander.
Sec. 21, Internal Security Act of 1950, 50 U.S.C. 797

While on this Installation all personnel and the property under their control are subject to search.

Content Consultant
Jerome Clark
Author, *The UFO Encyclopedia*
Former editor, *International UFO Reporter,*
published by the Center for UFO Studies

Core Library
An Imprint of Abdo Publishing
abdopublishing.com

abdopublishing.com

Published by Abdo Publishing, a division of ABDO, PO Box 398166, Minneapolis, Minnesota 55439. Copyright © 2016 by Abdo Consulting Group, Inc. International copyrights reserved in all countries. No part of this book may be reproduced in any form without written permission from the publisher. Core Library™ is a trademark and logo of Abdo Publishing.

Printed in the United States of America, North Mankato, Minnesota
072015
012016

THIS BOOK CONTAINS
RECYCLED MATERIALS

Cover Photo: Jon Elswick/AP Images
Interior Photos: Jon Elswick/AP Images, 1, 7, 12, 45; Cristina Muraca/Shutterstock Images, 4; Central Intelligence Agency, 9; Wally Fong/AP Images, 14; US Air Force, 17, 43; Warren K. Leffler/Library of Congress, 19; Frank R. Paul, 22; Public Domain, 25; iStockphoto, 26; AP Images, 30; Red Line Editorial, 31; World History Archive/Newscom, 33; Neil A. Armstrong/NASA/AP Images, 34; Central Intelligence Agency/Roadrunners Internationale, 36; Columbia Pictures/Photofest, 39

Editor: Mirella Miller
Series Designer: Ryan Gale

Library of Congress Control Number: 2015945989

Cataloging-in-Publication Data
Krasner, Barbara.
 The mystery of Area 51 / Barbara Krasner.
  p. cm. -- (Mysteries of history)
 ISBN 978-1-68078-022-2 (lib. bdg.)
 Includes bibliographical references and index.
 1. Unidentified flying objects--Sightings and encounters--Nevada--Juvenile literature. 2. Area 51 (Nev.)--Juvenile literature.   3. Air bases--Nevada--Juvenile literature. 4. Research aircraft--United States--Juvenile literature.   I. Title.
 001.942--dc23
                                                                         2015945989

CONTENTS

RESTAURANT
BAR · MOTEL

EARTHLINGS
WELCOME
LITTLE
ÁLÉÍNN

CHAPTER ONE

DREAMLAND

California author David Darlington had an appointment to keep. On an October day in 1993, he crossed the boundary between Nye and Lincoln counties in Nevada. He finally arrived at his destination, the small village of Rachel. There before him hung the red, white, and blue sign: "Earthlings Welcome: Little A'Le'Inn." The inn was

The Little A'Le'Inn welcomes guests from all around the world who want the chance to see unidentified flying objects near Area 51.

a modified house trailer. White plastic picnic tables dotted the parking lot.

Darlington had come to join a campout organized by Glenn Campbell, author of the *Area 51 Viewer's Guide*. Darlington found Campbell up the road in another house trailer. It was the Area 51 Research Center.

The Mystery of Area 51

Area 51 was rumored for years to be a secret air base. It was a place where weird events occurred: government experiments with nuclear bombs and sightings of unidentified flying objects (UFOs). Was Area 51 real?

Darlington had tried to piece together this puzzle. He first heard about Area 51 at a party before conducting some research on his own. He discovered that Area 51 was located next to the Nevada National Security Site, where the government had experimented with nuclear bombs since 1951. The area was called by many different code names: Groom

Area 51 is tightly monitored and secured so no one can enter without the correct security clearance.

Lake, Paradise Lake, Watertown, the Ranch, and Dreamland. No government agency officially admitted that Area 51 existed until many years later. According to the *Washington Post*, the name *Area 51* did not exist in 1995. An air force lawyer told a federal judge at the time: "There is no name for the operating location near Groom Lake."

Darlington and Campbell got on the road. They were in desert country. Eleven miles (18 km) out on the highway, they came upon a sign: "Warning: There is a restricted military installation to the West." They drove on and were met by the "Cammo Dudes," the name Campbell gave to Area 51 security guards for their camouflage outfits. They joined a group gathering for a hike to get a closer look from the point known as Freedom Ridge.

Area 51 did exist. It was there, physically. Area 51 stretched across 600 square miles (1,554 sq km) with the heaviest possible security. It lay 80 miles (129 km) north of Las Vegas, Nevada, and was surrounded by the Nevada National Security Site. Although a location this big must

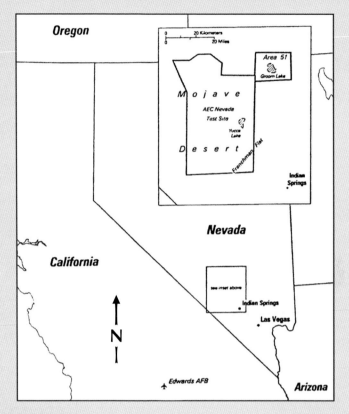

Area 51 Map

The Nevada National Security Site covers 1,360 square miles (3,522 sq km). It has been used by a number of government agencies to train people and to test equipment used to uncover weapons of mass destruction. This site includes Area 51. What do you notice about the placement of Area 51 within the site? How does the map explain why this site could be a good location for a secret air base?

have been difficult to hide, the government had mostly succeeded. The site belonged to the Atomic Energy Commission, now called the US Department of Energy.

Establishing Area 51

After World War II (1939–1945), the United States needed a place to test planes. These were not just any planes. President Dwight D. Eisenhower issued an order to find a secure place to test spy planes. These planes would monitor the Soviet Union's emerging nuclear weapons program. In early 1955, a group of men flew in a tiny aircraft over Nevada. This group included two Central Intelligence Agency (CIA) officers, Richard Bissell and Herbert Miller. Bissell was a former Yale economics professor who had been put in charge of the CIA spy plane project. Miller was the country's leading expert on Soviet nuclear weapons.

Bissell and Miller sighted what would become Area 51 from the sky. This would be the place to test the CIA's first spy plane, the U-2. As their plane descended, they saw evidence of a temporary landing strip. US Army Air Corps pilots had used it during World War II. Bissell recommended to President Eisenhower that he add a piece of adjoining land,

including Groom Lake,
to the Nevada National
Security Site to ensure
secrecy. Area 51 was born.

At Freedom Ridge

Campbell guided
Darlington and others on
foot to the lookout point,
Freedom Ridge. Many
people in Campbell's
group came here to
spot flying saucers,
or UFOs. They told of
their experiences with
aliens. They also told
stories of the base's 22
underground levels with
tunnels that connected
locations throughout

The Cold War

The United States emerged
from World War II as a
superpower. President
Eisenhower and other leaders
were concerned that the
Soviet Union, also one of the
war's victors, would spread its
belief in communism around
the world. They felt this
would threaten democracy.
Both the United States and
the Soviet Union believed the
other country had superior
weapons in development. The
Cold War between the United
States and the Soviet Union
erupted. Distrust grew, and in
the United States, Americans
had a real fear of Soviet
invasion and destruction. The
United States needed to be
prepared. Spy planes could
help produce the necessary
intelligence to prevent such
an attack.

A security vehicle monitors activity on Groom Road surrounding the mysterious Area 51.

the Southwest. The following morning, Darlington spotted groups of hangars, satellite dishes, four water tanks, a control tower, and other buildings. A five-story yellow hangar as big as a football field dwarfed everything.

By April 1995, Freedom Ridge was closed to the public. Campbell urged people who read his *Viewer's Guide* not to try to visit. Area 51 would remain a mystery.

Autobiographies of people involved with Area 51 can reveal much about decisions and activities. Consider the following from James R. Killian, First Special Assistant to President Eisenhower for Science and Technology:

> *After listening to our proposal and asking many hard questions, Eisenhower approved the development of the system, but he stipulated that it should be handled in an unconventional way so that it would not become entangled in the bureaucracy of the Defense Department or troubled by rivalries among the services. . . . Consequently, a special management arrangement was devised that made it possible for the advisory group of scientists and engineers constantly to appraise and guide the development program and to permit quick decisions to be made. The project was made the responsibility of the CIA.*
>
> *Source: James R. Killian Jr. Sputnik, Scientists, and Eisenhower: A Memoir of the First Special Assistant to the President for Science and Technology. Cambridge,MA: MIT Press, 1977. Print. 82.*

Back It Up

Killian uses evidence to support his point. Write a paragraph describing the point Killian is making. Then write down two or three pieces of evidence he uses to make his point.

SECRETS IN THE SKY

C ould the hangars that Darlington saw house secret aircraft? Under the blanket of night, Area 51 had conducted tests of secret aircraft since 1955. These aircraft projects were known as "black" projects. The Black Budget, the government's secret account for military and intelligence spending, funded the projects. Billions of dollars made up this budget.

Clarence "Kelly" Johnson, right, helped design and build the secret U-2 airplane.

The first black project at Area 51 was called Project Aquatone. Its mission was to build and test the U-2 airplane. The *U* stood for utility plane, a type of general aircraft, but it was hardly that. The plane would be used to secretly photograph Soviet missile bases. These photos could show US government leaders if and how the Soviet Union was preparing to attack. Aircraft manufacturer Lockheed Corporation, under the supervision of aerodynamics expert Clarence "Kelly" Johnson, would design and build the plane.

From the start, the U-2 would be unusual. Its super-long wings and aluminum exterior made it delicate and fast. The airplane would fly at record-breaking altitudes, more than 65,000 feet (19,810 m) high.

The first test flight took place in August 1955. Further tests stretched the plane's ability to soar at ever-increasing altitudes. Bissell, known to the Area 51

No air force in the world had reached the heights that the U-2 would.

men as Mr. B, was in charge. This meant the CIA, and not the US Air Force, led the project.

The air force's role was to fly pilots in from California to the Area 51 base on Monday morning and return to California on Friday evening. Mr. B did not want to arouse curiosity with cars coming in and out of the base. One Sunday night in November 1955, the U-2 project's security officer and four members of his staff boarded an Air Force C-54 transport plane in California. The plane never reached Area 51. It crashed into Mount Charleston, north of Las Vegas.

Francis Gary Powers

On May 1, 1960, CIA pilot Francis Gary Powers strapped into his U-2 cockpit. He had already flown 27 spy missions. His new mission was to take pictures of a Soviet missile base. He took off from Peshawar, Pakistan, and flew north to the Soviet Union. His flight would mark the CIA's deepest journey into the Soviet Union. After 90 minutes in the air, Powers was shot down by the Soviets. They put him on trial as a spy and sentenced him to ten years in prison. Powers was exchanged for a Soviet spy and returned to the United States in 1962.

No one survived the accident. The CIA rushed in to clean up the wreckage. Briefcases carrying secret documents had to be secured. The agency could not allow any evidence to be found.

Testing continued despite the crash. By January 1956, the U-2 was ready for action. It had the best camera lenses available. Plus, at an altitude of 72,000 feet (21,950 m), no other plane would be able to catch it while in flight.

Mr. B wanted to make sure the unique

Pilot Francis Gary Powers holds a model U-2 airplane as he sits through the 1962 hearings on the U-2 incident.

U-2, if sighted over Soviet territory, would not cause a stir. He developed a cover-up story stating the planes were used for high-altitude weather research. Although several people worked on this cover-up and approved its use, it would not persuade the Soviets.

More Black Projects

The CIA believed that after 18 to 25 months, the U-2 could be vulnerable to Soviet capture. Another plane would be needed then to both replace the

U-2 and escape Soviet radar detection. This new plane was code-named Project Oxcart, or the Archangel-12. It was to fly higher than the U-2—up to 97,000 feet (29,560 m) high, approximately three times higher than today's passenger airliners. The Archangel-12 would fly at speeds of 2,052 miles per hour (3,302 kmh), approximately four times faster than a passenger flight today.

Project Oxcart began in August 1959. It took three years for Lockheed to develop the design.

The first Archangel-12 was built in Burbank, California, taken apart, and sent to Area 51 in sections in early 1962. During its second test flight in May 1962, it traveled faster than the speed of sound.

Other black aircraft projects followed. One was the SR-71 Blackbird. Another was the F-117 Nighthawk stealth bomber, used in both the Persian Gulf War (1991) and the Iraq War (2003–2011).

FURTHER EVIDENCE

Chapter Two talks about the various types of airplanes tested at Area 51. Check out the website at the link below. Can you find information on the site that supports the author's point? Write a few sentences using information from the website as evidence to support the main point of this chapter.

U-2 and Oxcart Programs
mycorelibrary.com/area-51

The WAR of the WORLDS
By H. G. Wells

Author of "Under the Knife," "The Time Machine," etc.

CHAPTER THREE

STRANGE SIGHTINGS

Area 51 has developed a reputation for more than being a secret air base. It is also believed to be the site of UFOs. Reports of UFOs have filled newspapers since the 1800s. Some newspapers wondered whether Martians were responsible. In 1898 science fiction writer H. G. Wells published *The War of the Worlds*. In the book, he described a Martian invasion. Wells based his popular novel on reports of

The cover of the reprint version of *The War of the Worlds* depicted the Martian invasion Wells wrote about in the novel.

Martians and Martian canals that had been in recent scientific and popular news. The novel became a model of alien invasion movies of the mid-1900s and inspired a 1938 radio broadcast.

Charles Fort presented the first serious arguments in favor of the existence of UFOs between 1919 and 1932. His books were not commercially successful at the time of publication, but critics said later that he was ahead of his time. Fort said sightings happened all over the world. Moreover, he said, these kinds of fantastic things are common.

The War of the Worlds Radio Broadcast

On the night before Halloween in 1938, the Columbia Broadcasting System broadcast a version of H. G. Wells's novel of a Martian invasion, *The War of the Worlds*. A broadcaster broke into regularly scheduled programming and said listeners were about to hear a science fiction story. Few people paid attention to that statement. The live broadcast portraying an invasion of New Jersey and the attack on Earth sounded real to some people. The broadcast sparked mass panic.

Fort's books on UFOs and other unusual events continue to be popular decades after his death.

1947 and UFO Sightings

In June 1947, traveling salesman and pilot Kenneth Arnold spent an hour flying over Mount Rainier in Washington. He was searching for remains of a crashed military transport plane. Flashes of light caught his attention. At first he thought he was seeing a large flock of birds. Then he realized these

The city of Roswell, New Mexico, remembers the UFO crash that happened in 1947 with souvenir shops and UFO museums.

were solid objects, large and flat. He counted nine of them. Every few seconds, one of the objects would flip onto its side. Arnold thought they could be experimental jet planes. He calculated they were flying at approximately 1,700 miles per hour (2,740 kmh). To Arnold, the objects looked similar to saucers skipping across water. He shared what he saw with a newspaper reporter. The objects Arnold saw were given the name "flying saucers."

More than one week later, an odd crash occurred near Roswell, New Mexico, home of the Roswell Army Air Field. People believed a flying saucer had crashed. They also thought the US government was trying to hide the truth, the wreckage, and the bodies of the crew. People said the wreckage and the crew were taken to Area 51 through a series of underground tunnels. However, the wreckage was flown to Fort Worth Army Air Field and later to the Wright-Patterson Air Force Base in Dayton, Ohio.

What happened to the wreckage after that sparked speculation.

The US Army Air Forces said the crash was merely a failing weather balloon. But in 1978, more than 30 years later, two UFO researchers started asking questions in Roswell. People recalled a lot of military personnel arriving in town. They said they saw large boxes and child-sized bodies. The researchers came to the conclusion that the crew of the flying saucer was not of this world.

The US Government Responds

According to the CIA, UFO sightings increased with the testing of the high-altitude U-2 plane in the mid-1950s. After all, passenger planes at that time typically flew between 10,000 and 20,000 feet (3,050 and 6,100 m), and military aircraft flew at heights below 40,000 feet (12,190 m). Nothing had ever flown as high as a U-2 plane before. The plane's aluminum exterior glowed in the setting sun's reflection. Even airline pilots reported UFO sightings to air traffic controllers.

The US Air Force responded in 1948 by establishing a UFO investigative unit. Based at the Wright-Patterson Air Force Base, it collected information on the sightings. This became known as Project Blue Book. A UFO was defined as an aerial object or phenomenon the observer was unable to identify. This definition was later updated to an airborne object that did not look like any known aircraft or missile. The US Air Force tried to explain

This UFO report in Las Cruces, New Mexico, in 1967 was one of thousands the UFO investigative unit looked into between 1947 and 1969.

all sightings based on ordinary phenomena. The Project Blue Book investigators called on CIA staff in Washington, DC, to compare sightings with the U-2 flight logs. U-2 and A-12 flights accounted for more than half of the UFO reports during the late 1950s and 1960s. From the summer of 1947 until mid-December 1969, there were 12,618 official case reports of UFOs. Project Blue Book investigators could not confirm more than 700, or 6 percent, of the cases. However, knowledgeable observers rejected the CIA's analysis.

Year	Total Sightings	Unidentified Sightings
1947	122	12
1948	156	7
1949	186	22
1950	210	27
1951	169	22
1952	1,501	303
1953	509	42
1954	487	46
1955	545	24
1956	670	14
1957	1,006	14
1958	627	10
1959	390	12
1960	557	14
1961	591	13
1962	474	15
1963	399	14
1964	562	19
1965	887	16
1966	1,112	32
1967	937	19
1968	375	3
1969	146	1

Total UFO Sightings, 1947–1969

The US government set up an investigative unit in 1947 to monitor UFO activity. It operated for 22 years. From this chart, what patterns can you find about UFO sightings?

The CIA neither responded to critics nor produced any additional evidence. The investigative unit and the project closed down permanently in 1969. The investigation determined that no UFO sighting represented any threat.

Strange Happenings at Area 51

Area 51 did not exist in the late 1890s, or even in 1947. But in 1993, Glenn Campbell moved to Rachel, Nevada, from Boston, Massachusetts. Since then, Rachel has attracted people who want to see UFOs and catch a glimpse of Area 51. In October 2008, UFO hunter William J. Birnes and his crew met up with Campbell, who led them to an Area 51 lookout point. There they observed an unusually large, recently constructed hangar on the Area 51 base. With a surveillance camera, they were able to capture an image of a UFO. They could not determine whether it belonged to the United States or even Earth.

Other strange phenomena have been associated with Area 51. There are reports of human and

This satellite picture of Area 51 shows little detail as to what actually happens at the secret air base.

extraterrestrial cloning at Area 51. Some people believe that Area 51 reverse engineers alien spaceships to figure out how the machines work. Further, some people insist that Neil Armstrong and Buzz Aldrin never set foot on the moon in 1969. They say the moon landing was staged at Area 51 and was a trick to get the Soviet Union to believe the United

Some Americans believed the 1969 US moon landing was fake and staged in a studio.

States' space program was more advanced. There is little evidence for these theories about Area 51, but the beliefs persist.

UFO sightings increased after Area 51 opened. Here, the CIA explains reports of UFOs from pilots:

> *Such reports were most prevalent in the early evening hours from pilots of airliners flying from east to west. . . . Not only did the airline pilots report their sightings to air traffic controllers, but they and ground-based observers also wrote letters to the Air Force unit at Wright Air Development Command. . . . Investigators regularly called on the [Central Intelligence] Agency's Project Staff in Washington to check reported UFO sightings against U-2 flight logs. This enabled the investigators to eliminate the majority of the UFO reports, although they could not reveal to the letter writers the true cause of the UFO sightings.*
>
> Source: Gregory W. Pedlow and Donald E. Welzenbach. "The Central Intelligence Agency and Overhead Reconnaissance: The U-2 and OXCART Programs, 1954–1974." Central Intelligence Agency. Central Intelligence Agency, 1998. Web. Accessed May 27, 2015.

What's the Big Idea?

Take a close look at this passage. What is the main point being made by the CIA? Find two or three supporting details. Explain how these details support the main idea.

SOLVING THE MYSTERY

For more than 50 years, Area 51 had been cloaked in mystery. But in 2005, the CIA declassified its 1998 report about the U-2 and Project Oxcart programs. However, the report was heavily edited. Even the table of contents had large portions blacked out. A similar report from 1992 of nearly 400 pages was declassified in 2013. Fewer portions were blacked out. Most importantly,

In 2014 the CIA took responsibility for strange objects in the sky during the 1950s, which could have included A-12 airplanes.

it admitted the existence of Area 51 by name. Both reports had originally been marked Secret. Getting the CIA to make these reports public was the work of Jeffrey T. Richelson of the National Security Archives in Washington, DC. He requested an Area 51 map and other documents in 2005 through the Freedom of Information Act. He was studying aerial surveillance programs. The map confirmed the location of Area 51, while the documents detailed the surveillance programs.

Researchers had long known about Area 51. The critical factor was

Aliens have been featured in many movies throughout the decades, including the *Men in Black* movies.

The World of Ufologists

The term "ufologist" refers to someone who researches UFOs through physical evidence, visual evidence, reports, and other sources. Since the reported 1947 sightings, organizations have formed to bring ufologists together for a common purpose. One of the organizations is the Center for UFO Studies. It was founded in 1973 by J. Allen Hynek of Northwestern University's Astronomy Department. He also served as a consultant to Project Blue Book. Each year on July 2, World UFO Day takes place across the globe. Its goal is to raise awareness of UFOs and to get the government to release documents about UFOs.

that now, the CIA owned up to its existence. The release of the report also laid to rest the stories of spaceships and aliens. The CIA tweeted on December 29, 2014: "#1 most read on our #Bestof2014 list: Reports of unusual activity in the skies in the '50s? It was us." This message was retweeted almost 2,000 times and made headlines.

Some Questions Are Answered

Area 51's past has been acknowledged. Its connection to aliens from outer space has been featured in movies. *Area 51* is also the name of a combat video game introduced in 2005. The game's plot is based on the 1947 Roswell, New Mexico, crash. It imagines that aliens were taken to Area 51.

Although some information has been revealed, questions about Area 51 still remain. Current activities at Area 51 are not public knowledge. When journalists visit the site and try to dig deep into the truth, they are simply told, "You don't have a need to know."

EXPLORE ONLINE

Chapter Four discusses UFO sightings and their relationship to Area 51. It mentions Project Blue Book. The website below also provides information on Project Blue Book. Find a line or two from this website that relates to the information in the chapter. Does it support the chapter? Or does it add a new piece of evidence?

Project Blue Book
mycorelibrary.com/area-51

Area 51 is a top secret air base.

Evidence for:

- The CIA's declassified reports, especially the one released in 2013, admit to the existence of Area 51.
- Memoirs of people who had a role in Area 51's development, such as James Killian, prove its existence.

Evidence against:

- Rumors of secret aircraft and alien spaceships could all be a cover-up by the US government.

Area 51 is a place of secret UFO and alien activity.

Evidence for:

- Glenn Campbell's *Area 51 Viewer's Guide* and the gathering of people to catch sight of UFOs around the base suggest actual sightings.
- Bob Lazar's report claimed he worked at Area 51.

Evidence against:

- The CIA's declassified reports explain that the majority of UFO sightings were really CIA aircraft.

- Stanton T. Friedman debunked Bob Lazar's report.
- The number of sightings and the number of flying objects that could not be identified by Project Blue Book are small.

Area 51 remains an unsolved mystery.

Evidence for:
- Journalists are denied entry.
- Large structures, such as a hangar, have recently been built.

Evidence against:
- The CIA's declassified information has revealed some information.

STOP AND THINK

Why Do I Care?

Maybe you do not believe in UFOs or aliens. But that doesn't mean you can't learn more about the mystery of Area 51. Chapter Four shows how Jeffrey Richelson used the Freedom of Information Act to get the CIA to release Area 51 reports. He had to wait a long time. What information would you ask for from the government? Why?

Take a Stand

Chapter Three discusses UFO hunters. Some observers believed spaceships could be the only explanation for the lights they observed. Others believed what they saw must have been experimental airplanes. Do you think these people saw UFOs? Or do you think it could have been U-2 or A-12 planes flying through the sky? Why?

Say What?

Studying Area 51 can mean learning a lot of new vocabulary. Find five words in this book you've never heard before. Use a dictionary to find out what they mean. Then write the meanings in your own words, and use each word in a new sentence.

You Are There

Imagine you were a U-2 pilot. What thoughts would go through your mind as you prepared for flight? What do you think it feels like to fly so high in the air and at such fast speeds? Write a letter to your friends telling them what it is like. Be sure to add plenty of detail to your notes.

GLOSSARY

aerodynamics
a science that studies how objects move through air

clearance
authorization to classified information

cloning
producing an exact copy of another person or thing

declassified
allowing the public to see or learn about something that was secret

extraterrestrial
a being that comes from or exists somewhere other than Earth

flight logs
written records of flights, including dates and takeoff times

hangar
a building where aircraft are kept

missile
a weapon that is thrown, shot, or launched

reverse engineer
to study the parts of something to see how it was made and how it works in order to make something similar

surveillance
close and continuous observation of a person, group, object, or area

LEARN MORE

Books

Higgins, Nadia. *Area 51*. Minneapolis: Bellwether Media, 2014.

Martin, Ted. *Area 51*. Minneapolis: Bellwether Media, 2012.

Perish, Patrick. *Are UFOs Real?* Mankato, MN: Amicus, 2014.

Websites

To learn more about Mysteries of History, visit **booklinks.abdopublishing.com**. These links are routinely monitored and updated to provide the most current information available.

Visit **mycorelibrary.com** for free additional tools for teachers and students.

INDEX

ABOUT THE AUTHOR

Barbara Krasner is a freelance children's author who enjoys writing about history. She is particularly interested in the 1950s and the Cold War. She lives in New Jersey and teaches writing at a local university.